THE ART OF CHILDREN PHOTOGRAPHY

Hector M. Melendez

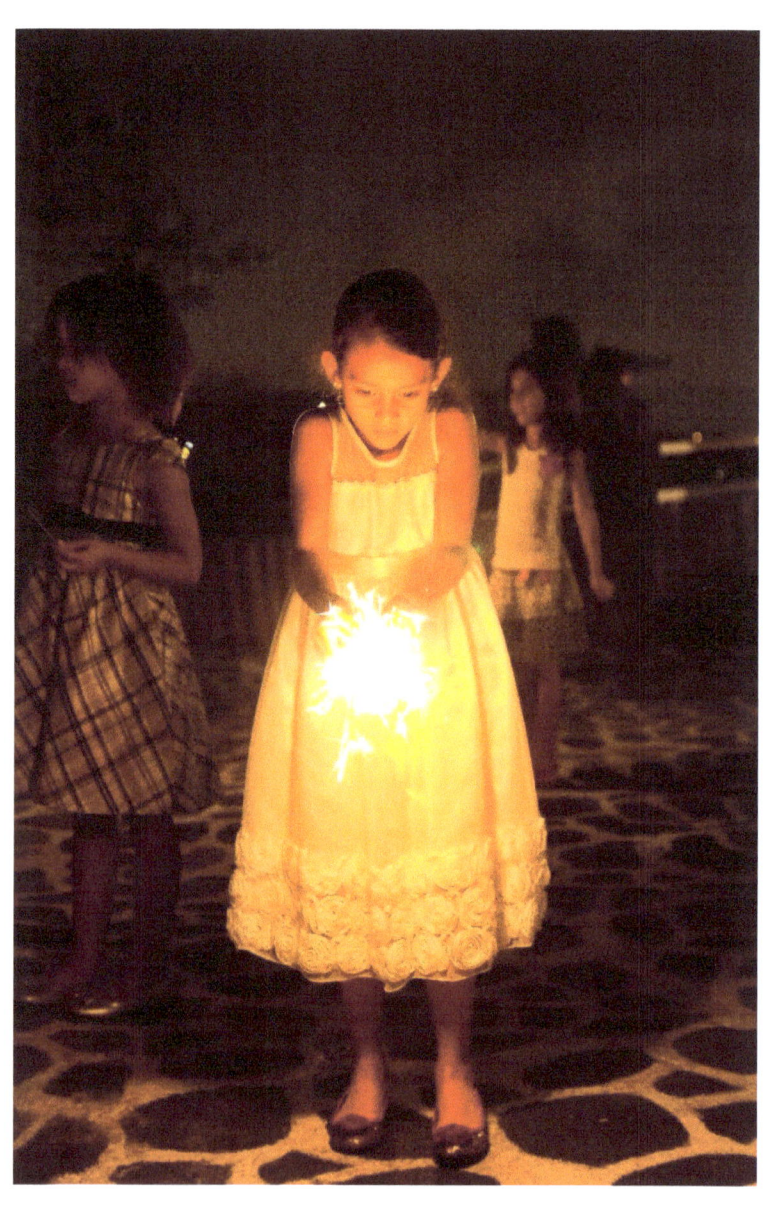

Copyright © 2020 Moicam Photography

Contents

INTRODUCTION 4

TODDLERS 6

GROWNUPS 11

ACTION 13

LINES, TRIANGLES AND RULE OF THIRDS 16

EVENTS 18

TIMID CHILDREN 20

TEENS 22

LIGHT 24

TIPS TO TAKE GREAT PHOTOS 26

EQUIPMENT 30

CONTINGENCY PLANNING 31

EDITING 33

FINAL PRODUCT 35

INTRODUCTION

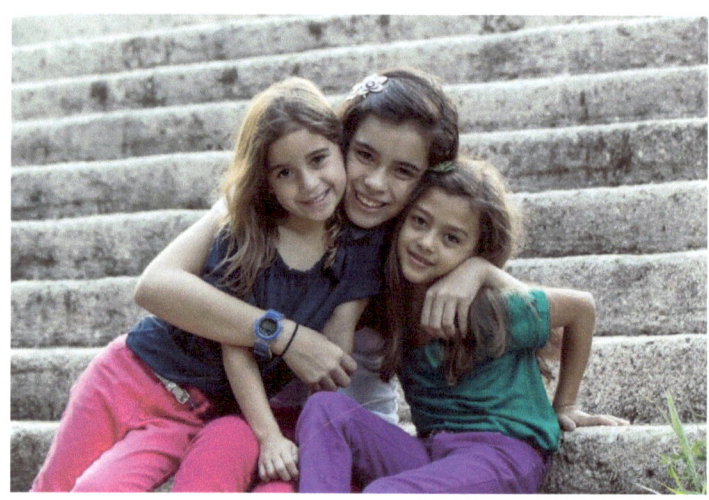

My interest in photography began with landscapes. Being a resident of the Caribbean island of Puerto Rico, and having so many beautiful landscapes such as beaches, rain forest, rivers, and mountains, helped develop my eye for this art. It was not until the birth of my first child that I entered the world of children photography, my children being the best motivation to read books, take courses and practice. I decided to practice with my friend's children and in a short time I began to be referred to do work for other people, this being my starting point in the photography business. In this book I share my techniques to take great photos of children. This book is aimed at people with basic knowledge in photography. I recommend people who are starting to use a DSLR camera to buy a basic photography book and learn how to use your camera in manual mode first. I hope you enjoy and learn reading this book.

TODDLERS

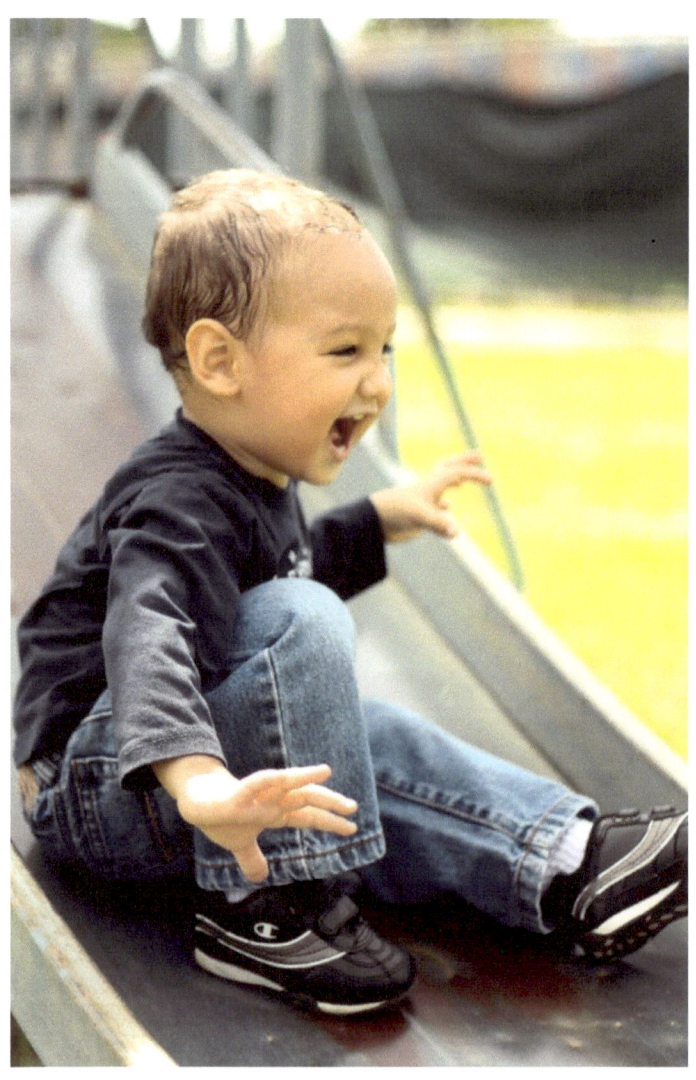

Babies grow fast, and parents want to capture a moment in time before they grow. Toddlers are less aware of the camera, making it easier to take joyful and spontaneous moments, especially when they are outdoors exploring their surroundings.

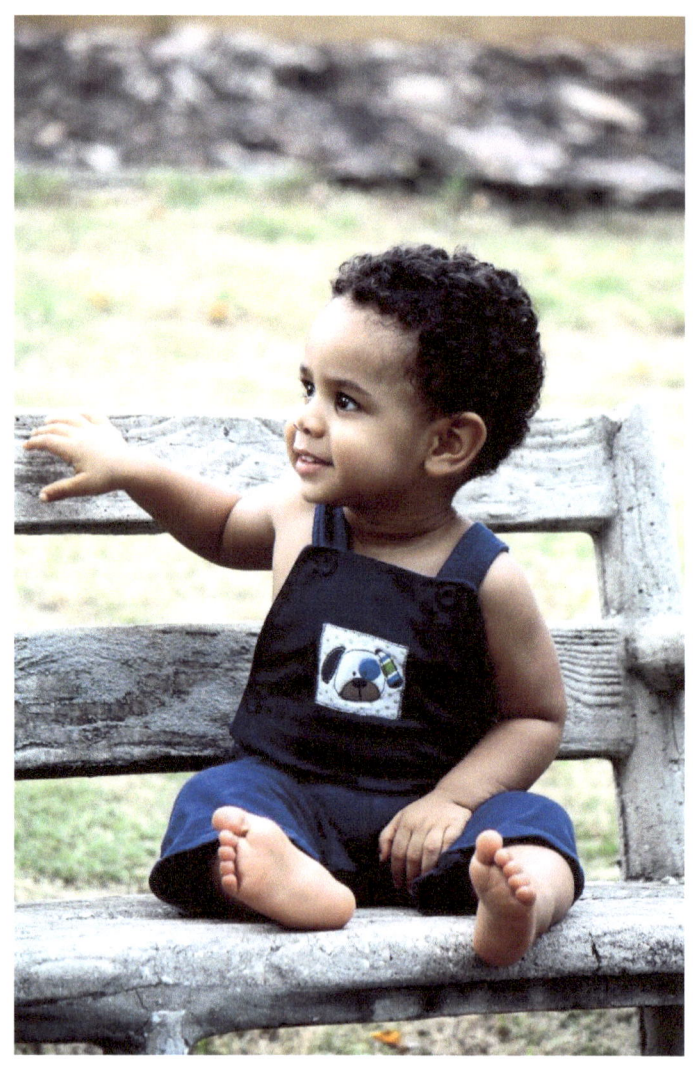

We must be a bit far so that they are not aware of our presence and can express themselves. Bare feet are a good idea somewhere in the session.

For these little kids we must be kneeling to be at their level.

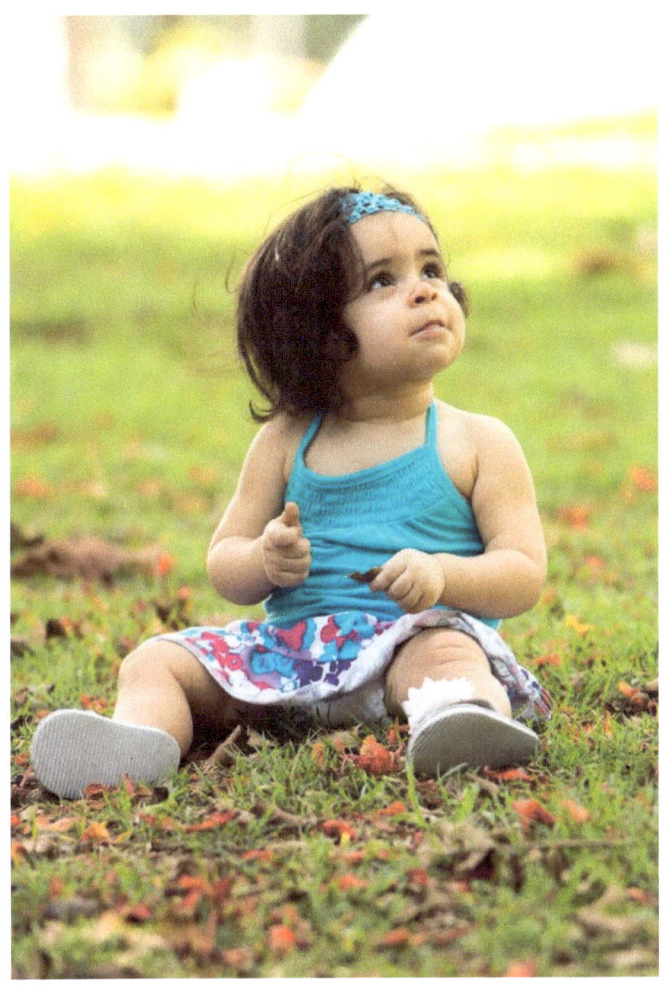

To have a successful session, it is important to position them in interesting places. Have your eye always on the camera so you do not miss the moment.

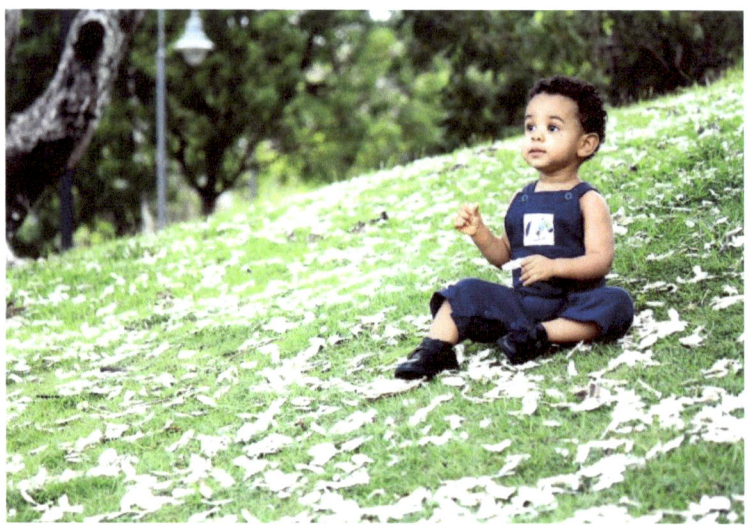

GROWNUPS

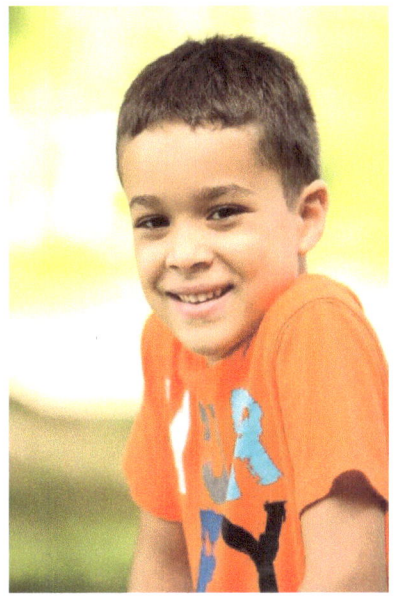

Getting confidence from young children before and during the session is essential because they already know that a stranger is going to take pictures of them. We should talk with them about things they like (favorite video games or dolls). At the beginning of the session, let us take a few pictures to show the children how cool they look on the camera screen. This technique works very well so that they lose shyness and want to be main characters of a great photography session, as you can see in the next page, where after seeing several photos the, child began to show off with his

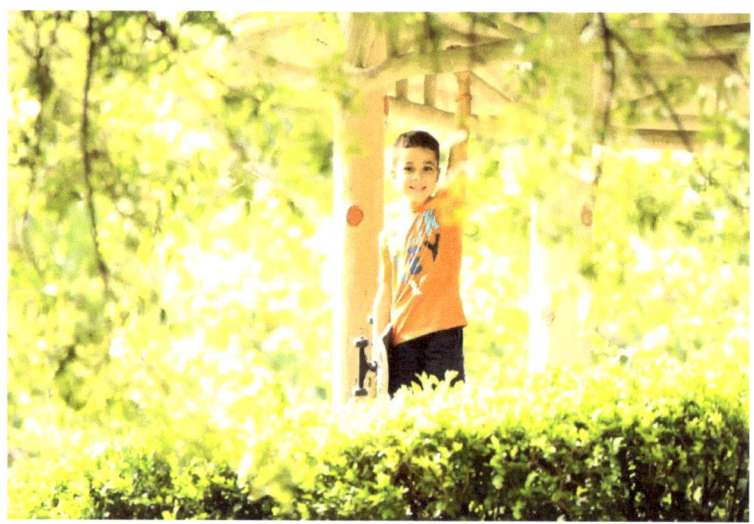

skateboard, and later in the session we achieved a photo like the one in this page, a completely natural expression.

Once we gain this confidence, the session will continue very smoothly. Continue to work with a super telephoto lens so that there is no close intimidation.

ACTION

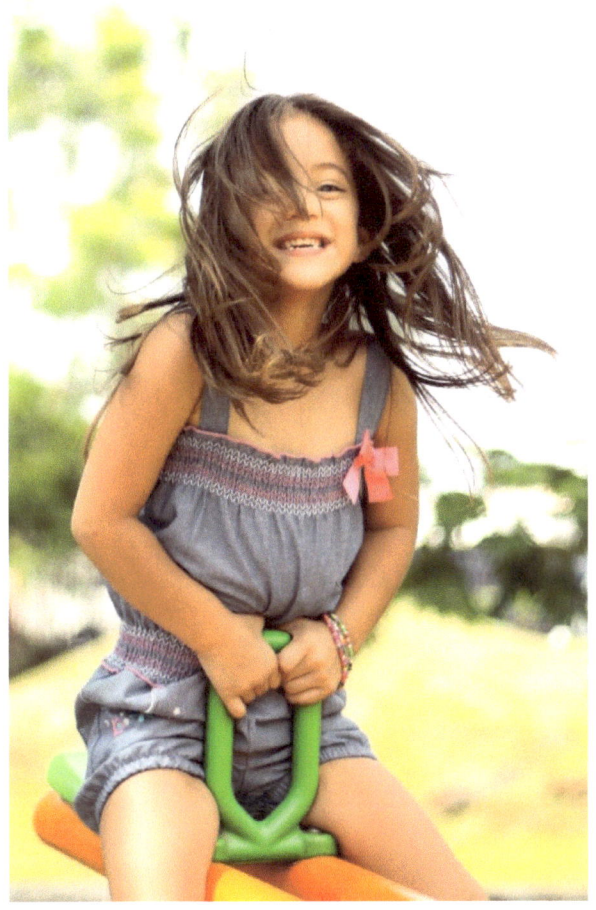

Sometimes we must take quick moments, as in this photo. The camera must be in burst mode and at a fast speed (approximately 1/500 onwards) to freeze the moment and have the image as sharp as possible. In this image the photos were taken when the girl was going down, achieving the effect on her hair floating in the air. The best of several photos of that moment was selected to deliver to their parents in the final product.

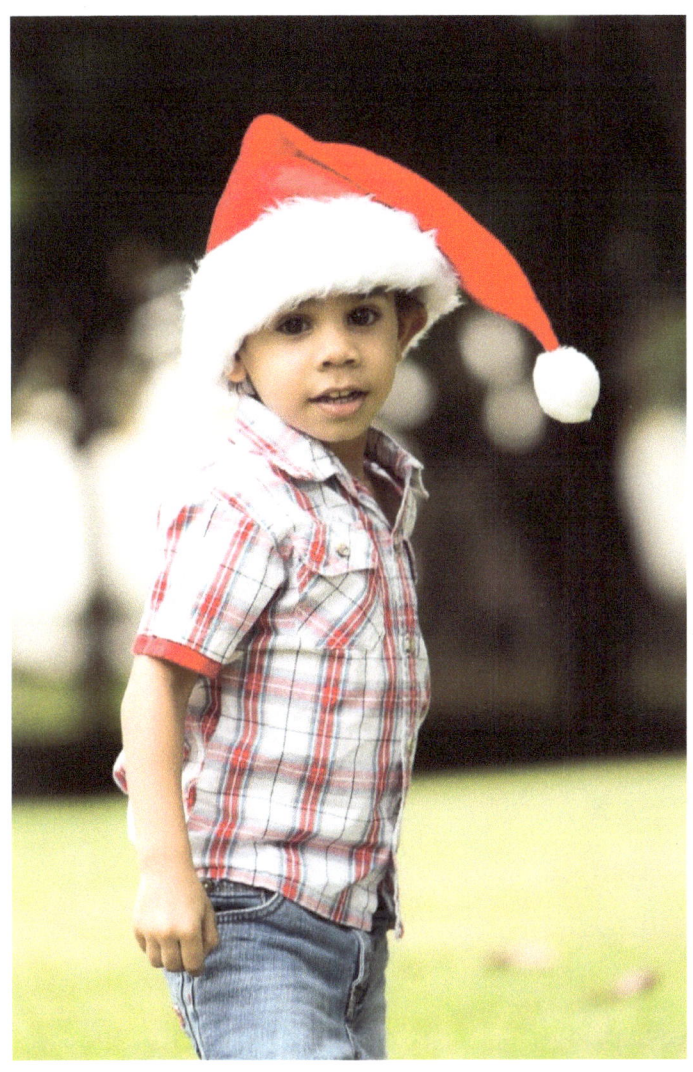

A head movement was frozen in this image as you can see in the Santa hat.

LINES, TRIANGLES AND RULE OF THIRDS

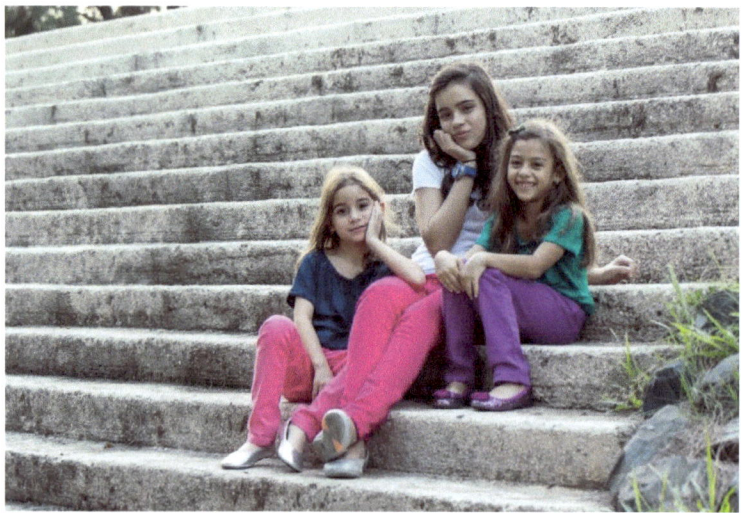

 Finding diagonal lines helps us a lot as is the case of this photo, where the stairs form diagonals lines and practically none is perfectly horizontal.

The photo was taken at an angle for that same purpose. The girls were positioned forming a triangle, and I waited for the perfect moment to take the picture. The wear of the stairs gives them a touch of old age, which helps make the image more interesting. I left some space to the left to apply the rule of thirds for this image.

EVENTS

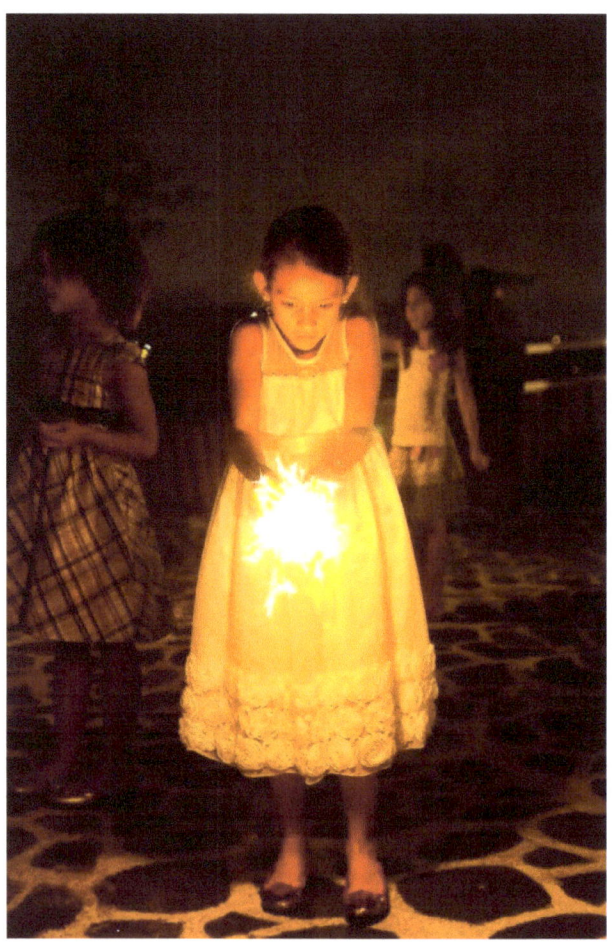

In wedding events there are always children, and it is always good to be aware when they become active. At a time that was passive inside the premises the children were having fun outside playing with star lights. I took advantage of the situation without them noticing. I took several photos without flash. Newlyweds will always be grateful for these moments to be captured.

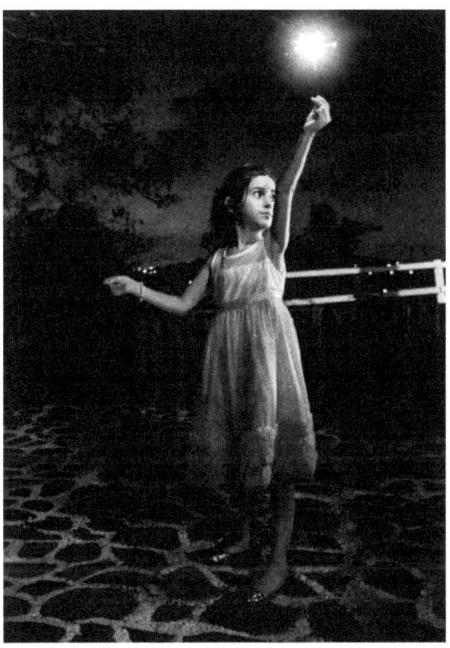

The girls' attire makes this moment timeless.

TIMID CHILDREN

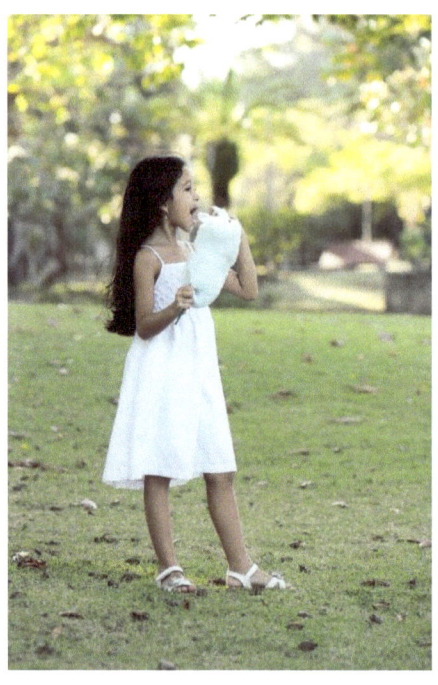

Sometimes children just do not want to cooperate. In these cases, you need to have a little more patience because we must lengthen the session a little bit and achieve good images when children are not aware of

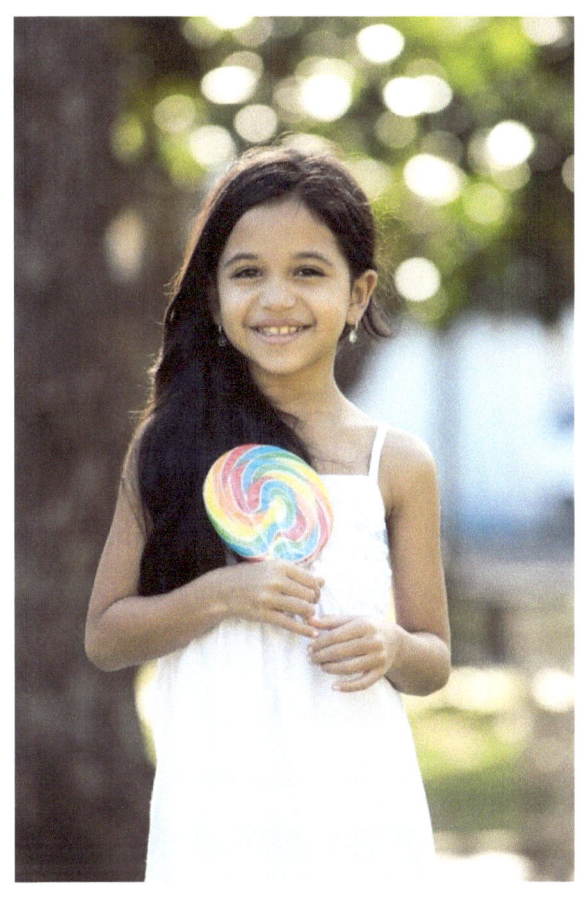

the camera, like the first image in this chapter. Candies can be helpful in these cases. Later in the session this young girl peeks at the camera. This image was achieved because of the distance between her and me.

TEENS

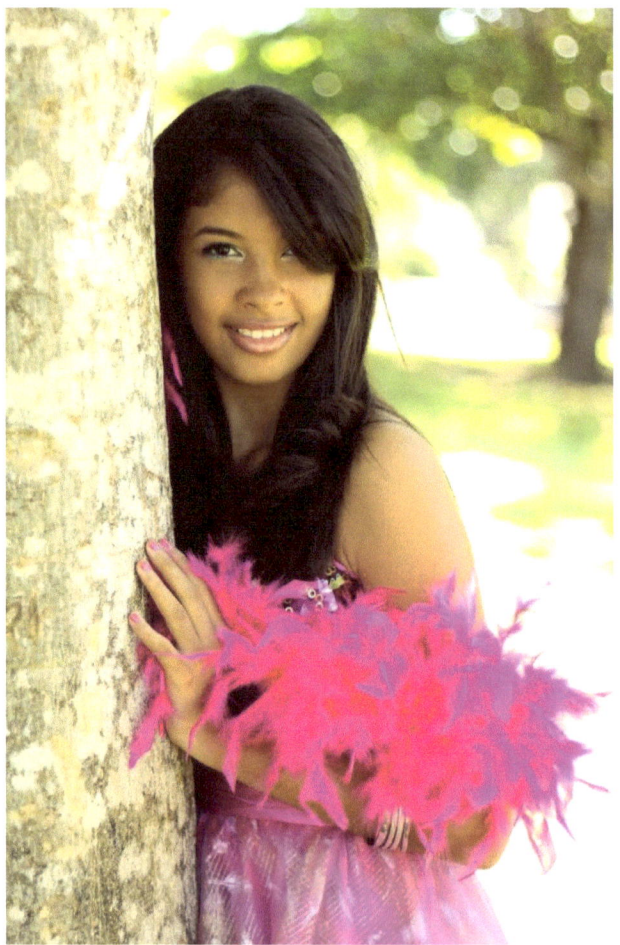

Teens can be much more cooperative, since they want to look good. They want to do their own poses and you just must help them a bit to refine.

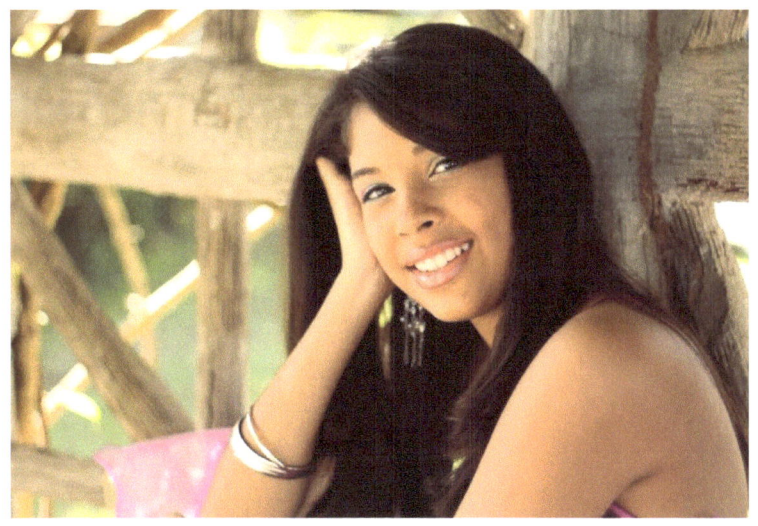

Whenever we pose them, try to make them look comfortable. Their body should be relaxed, and the smile needs to look natural. Telling them some good jokes should help us achieve our mission for natural facial expressions.

LIGHT

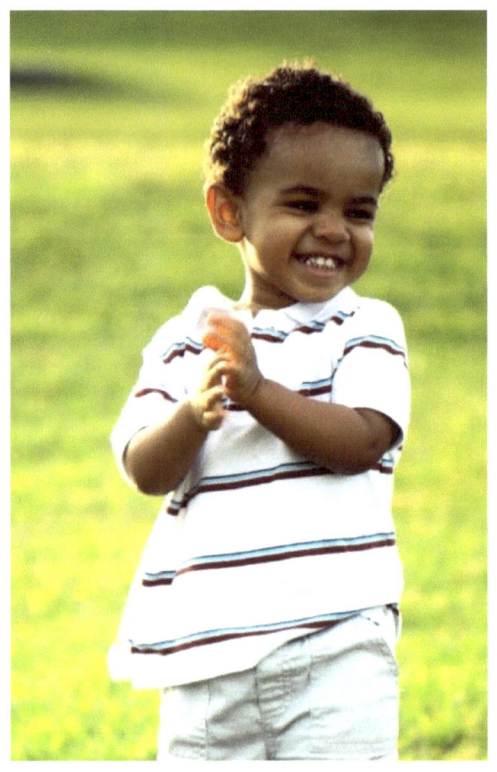

Always remember to do your sessions in the afternoon. Try to start three hours before sunset. The more the sun falls, the warmer the colors. This way we have no unwanted shadows and flat colors of the midday sun. It is important to use the light that enters between the trees to our favor. This way, when we throw the background out of focus, it can look remarkably interesting.

I do not use flash for any of my children's sessions because I do my sessions with good sun light and because I am far from my subjects. Try to position your subjects with the sun lighting their back. This way we can achieve dramatic images.

TIPS TO TAKE GREAT PHOTOS

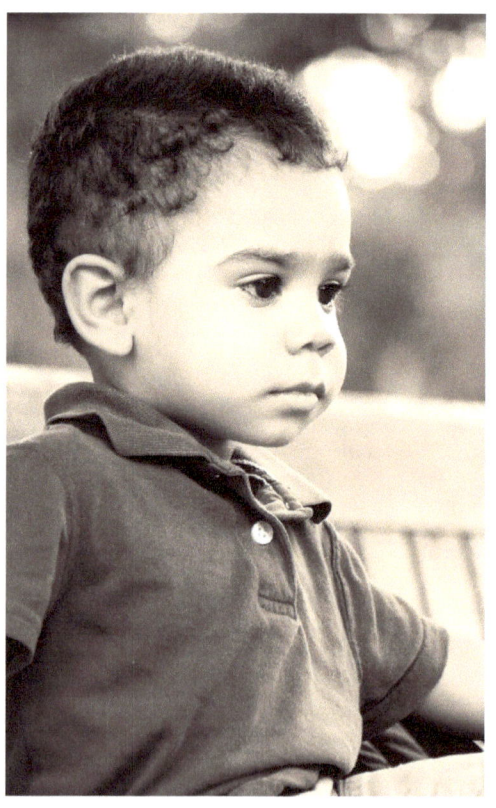

Let us always work with the camera in burst mode. This way we try not to miss the perfect moment. We should never be worried about running out of memory. These days memory cards are quite economical. Buy memory cards with enough space and always have backup.

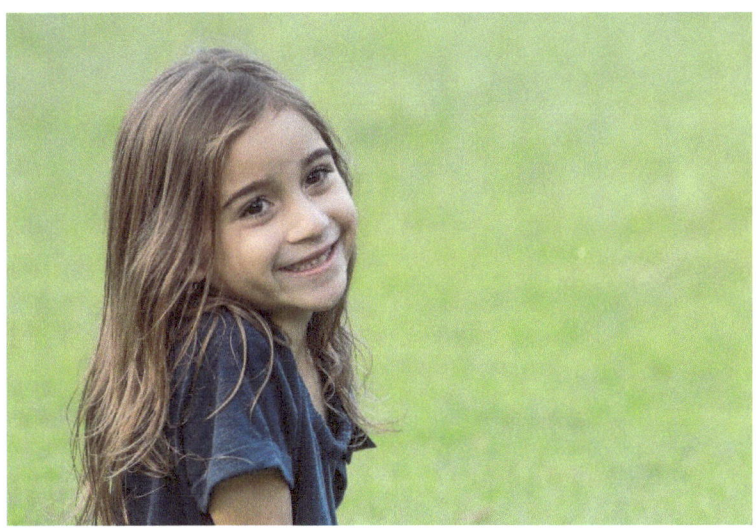

For me it is important that our images look clean. There must be the least number of objects that distract the eye of the viewer. There should be no people other than our subjects. It should appear that our subjects are alone in the photo. That is why throwing the background out of focus is important. This makes our subjects the main character. Less is more. Try to take almost every image with the lens at its maximum focal length to throw the background out of focus.

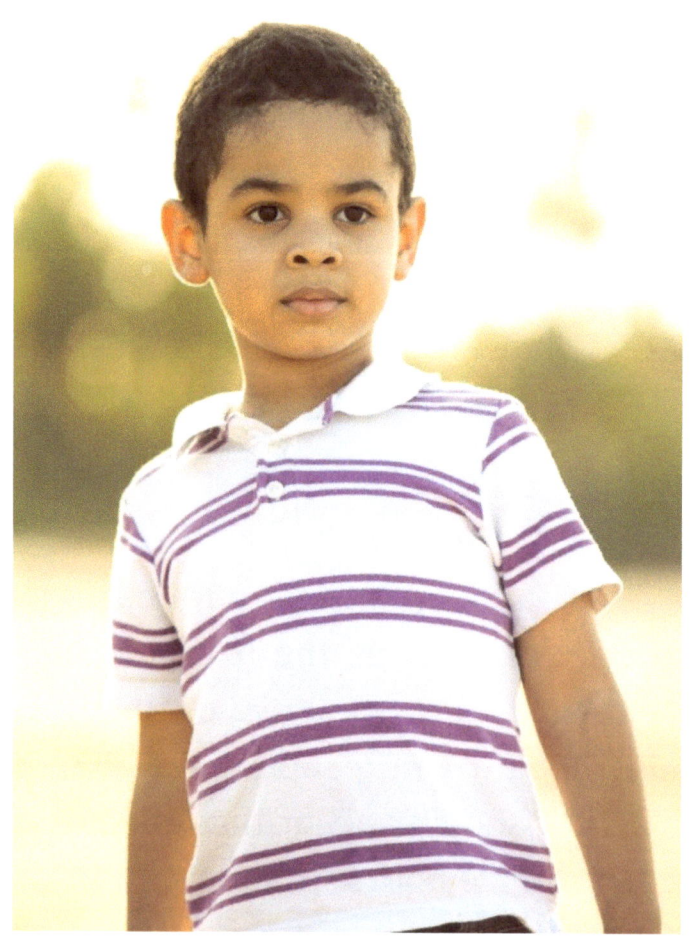

Use the spot meter in your camera to measure light with a neutral color, like the green of the grass. Be aware of changing light and measure again if needed.

Always be prepared for the moment having both hands on the camera. Compose with your eye carefully and take the images. This way we avoid spending more time editing. Remember that cropping too much reduces image resolution.

EQUIPMENT

- Two DSLR cameras
- Super Telephoto 70-200mm (for full size sensor camera) or 50-150mm (for APS-C sensor camera) with 2.8 fixed aperture at any distance, and image stabilization
- Backup lens
- Battery grip for more energy time and better camera handling
- Two memory cards with space for at least 1,000 images each
- Lens cleaning kit
- Lens hood

CONTINGENCY PLANNING

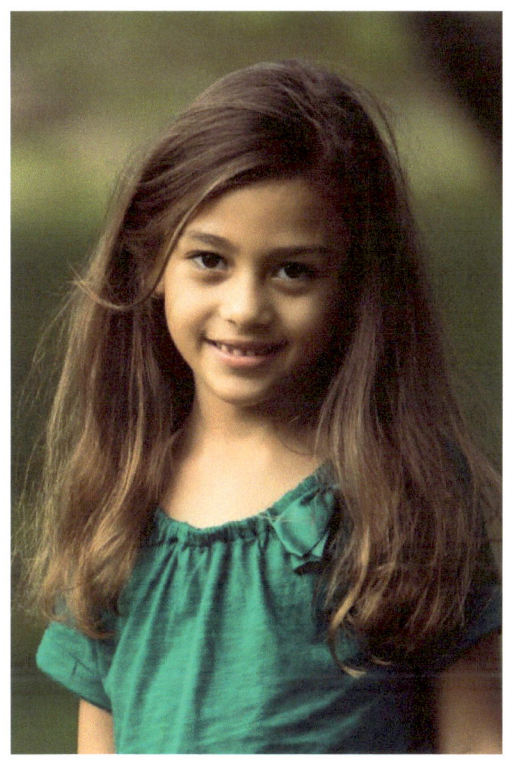

Making backup on a computer, external disk drive and in a cloud service, the same day of the session, is a must. When editing, make backup of your work at the end of the day.

This way we avoid losing our work in the event of any accident.

EDITING

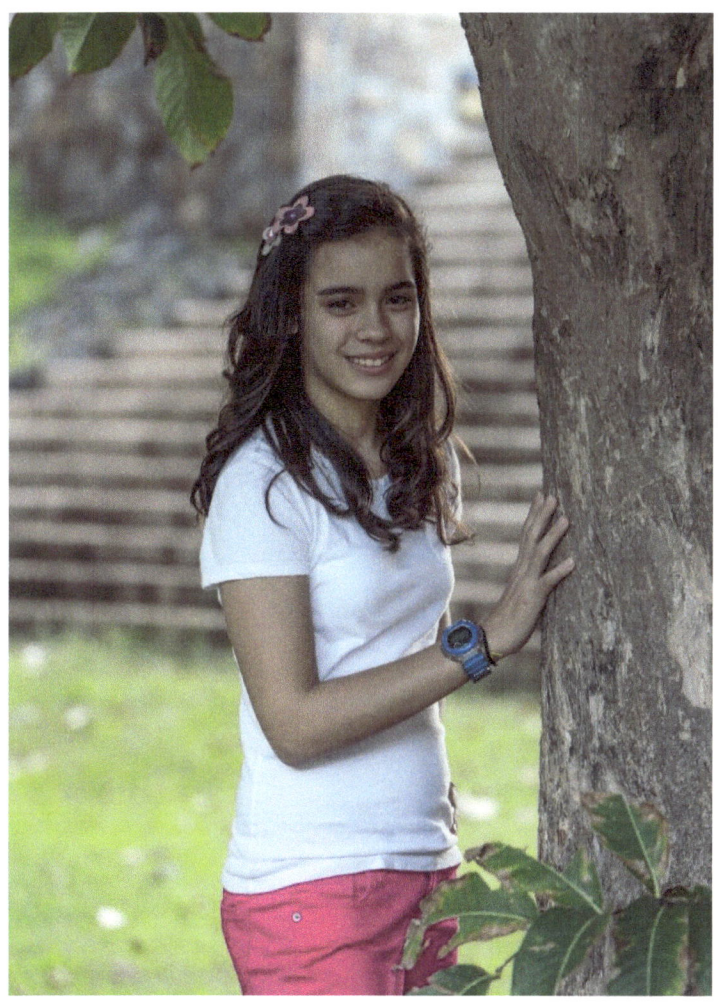

My advice is to take all our photos in RAW format. This way we will have more control when editing. We can crop, adjust white balance, raise, or lower up to two full stops in case we miss the correct exposure due to light changes, and we can adjust shadows, highlights, and colors. Photos in jpeg format are not very manageable. Use a good desktop computer application for handling RAW photos format.

After we finish editing, we convert to jpeg format for the final product.

FINAL PRODUCT

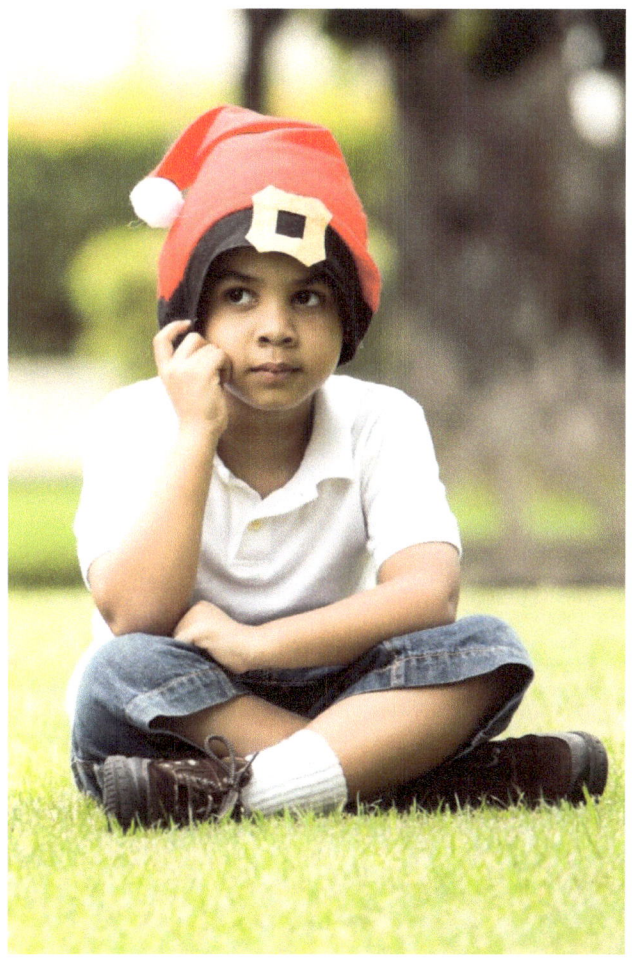

Since in my children's sessions I always work with my camera in burst mode, I can end up with around 500 photos per session. Already sitting in front of my computer I start selecting the photos that artistically meet my requirements, and then I start editing. I deliver around 35 color images with copies in black and white, in a well-presented device.

On the internet we can find several photography companies that help us with interesting quality items and devices to store photos.

www.ingramcontent.com/pod-product-compliance
Lightning Source LLC
Chambersburg PA
CBHW040340220526
45473CB00009B/2744